IN THE SECRET OF MY HEART

IN THE SECRET OF MY HEART

Moments of Stillness in the Heart of Christ

Anna Burke

VERITAS

Published 2010 by
Veritas Publications
7–8 Lower Abbey Street
Dublin 1
Ireland
publications@veritas.ie
www.veritas.ie

ISBN 978 1 84730 243 4

10 9 8 7 6 5 4 3 2 1

A catalogue record for this book is available from the British Library.

Designed by Tanya M. Ross
Printed in Ireland by Hudson Killeen, Dublin

Veritas books are printed on paper made from the wood pulp of
managed forests. For every tree felled, at least one tree is planted,
thereby renewing natural resources.

This book is dedicated to the men and women who understand that 'mine is yours'. They light the fire and make the tea for all who pass by, and in the secret of their hearts they hold a well.

In the Secret of My Heart is especially dedicated to Christine Burke.

CONTENTS

INTRODUCTION

On 27 January 2006, Pope Benedict XVI issued his first Encyclical Letter, *Deus caritas est* – *God is love*. The letter was awaited with great interest and welcomed with great joy. Pope Benedict had reached into the heart of the matter, reminding us that love is the basic tenet of Christianity and the message most urgently needed today. The Pope's moving reflection on love has helped the Catholic Church to retrieve its dignity and restore its splendour.

In the Secret of My Heart is a prayer book inspired by the beauty of *Deus caritas est*. The title reflects the Pope's teaching that love is indeed 'the heart' of Christian faith. This prayer book is structured according to scriptural themes, offering prayers for reflective times together with intercessory and communal prayers. The founding symbol for these reflections is the Sacred Heart of Jesus, a timeless image of divine love in a human heart.

THE HEART ENCOUNTERS

Being Christian is not the result of an ethical choice or a lofty idea, but the encounter with an event, a person, which gives life a new horizon and a decisive direction.

(Deus caritas est, Introduction)

AT THE WELL:
Jesus said to her, 'Give me a drink of water'. (John 4:7)

O woman of the well, you know about walking for water. You know about walking in the rising sun as you repeat the daily observance of drawing from the well. With your breath you are faithful to filling and to emptying, every day, for all of your life.

Jesus saw her that day with her empty bucket. She had formed an intimate connection: the woman, the bucket and the well, and so she had become the carrier of water. It was her timeless ritual to search for water. He counted the trips that the woman had made, a million in one lifetime just to find water to ease the thirst and to keep hope in the village. Her feet were worn with walking, their skin baked dry and split open. He saw her that day as she prepared again to raise the bucket skyward, its water spilling out onto the parched earth. She was numbed with ritual, numbed with walking and carrying, with bending and lifting, with returning and starting again. Her love had gone unnoticed and she was dry with longing.

She did not face him but she could feel his presence in the morning sunshine. He was a Jew and apart from the fatigue of weary travellers, the law decreed that they had nothing else in common. Her heart welcomed the distance that tradition provided and she lowered her bucket another time. But the man from Galilee had seen the woman from Samaria. She had continued the journey for the sake of the water. She was like him, being full of hunger, full of thirst, full of searching and of emptying. On her head she carried a bucket full of service. He recognised the story and he moved closer to the well.

As she turned to leave the well that day the man called out to the woman, 'Give me a drink'.

We Pray:

> Lord, give us the water of life,
> Lead us to living springs.
> Lord, quench the thirst of our hearts,
> Lead us to living springs.
> Lord, fill our empty buckets with healing and with hope,
> Lead us to living springs.
>
> O love of God in the heart of Jesus, meet us at the well of our longings and ease our thirst in the spring of living water. We place all our trust, O God, in your love. Amen.

AT THE FUNERAL:
Jesus said, 'Young man! Get up, I tell you!' The dead man sat up and began to talk and Jesus gave him back to his mother. (Luke 7:14-15)

I had watched you struggle with his sickness and death, and then you faced the day when you had to let him go. I could feel the slowing down of your heart and the closing down of your feelings. You had told yourself that it couldn't happen and that it wouldn't happen, but death moved steadily into his body, ignoring your pleas, forgetting the devastation. I remember the day as you remember the day. A strange and dark silence settled on the hillside; the wind cried in the trees and the birds refused to fly. The words of comfort from your closest friend were distant and fatiguing. You didn't cry on that last breath; you just stopped thinking. I remember crying for you on that day and holding your heart safely in my own heart.

The funeral procession was long and arduous, the warm dust clung to our lips and smarted our eyes. I saw your heavy step, your bowed head and veiled face. You were alone and yet your faith whispered, 'Not my will'. The words took my breath away. I knew what it asked: to dig down, so deeply into the last reserves of holding on. I hastened my step and soon I was walking beside you, shoulder to shoulder. You took my hand and placed it in yours and together we touched the bier. In this encounter I felt your faith stirring in my veins and your love tugging at my heart. The heavens began to open and a soft breeze carried a stream of light across the valley. The dead hand moved and then it opened. I raised him up and returned him to you.

We Pray:

For faith to break through barriers and come to you,
Lord, touch us and let us go free.
For hope in the beginning time and in the end time,
Lord, touch us and let us go free.
For health and strength to live life fully,
Lord, touch us and let us go free.

O love of God in the heart of Jesus, you found me in my lowest place and you walked beside me into the night. I held on to you and the morning broke with splendour. I place all my trust in your love. Amen.

AT THE LAKE:
They left their nets on the shore and followed him. (Luke 5:11)

Jesus believed in invitations and he drew people from their market places to follow the dream of shared bread and gentle hearts. His invitation was given to women and men, to shepherds and kings. It was an invitation to love magnanimously, to give and to forgive. In this moment when hearts came face to face, the question for many became irresistible. The fishermen left their nets and the women left their water buckets. The tax collectors left their earnings and the dead left their graves. Centurions and Samaritans, Pharisees and Levites were also on the guest list and the fig tree and the growing seeds heard the call rumbling in the soil, urging them to fruitfulness. People still abandon their nets for the freedom of the ocean, to journey into the heart of God.

When Peter and Andrew met the stranger on the shore the men had no way of knowing where this encounter would take them. He would lead them to a new experience of life, to dreams beyond all telling, to be partners in the reshaping of history. Fishermen were an unlikely choice in the fulfilment of a divine plan, but Jesus came with a purpose of universal salvation, to raise humankind to become a new creation. The men in the boats were drawn into the encounter. Some people do that – they ask a different question and invite us to cross the frontier. Encounters of the Galilee kind have life-altering possibility, moments of personal emotion and of world vision. The men in the boats had left their nets.

Love is like that; it calls us beyond ourselves and reveals the expanse of a human response. It awakens the greatness of our generosity and our capacity for life on the front. The history of the universe is an epic charged with love's response and Peter and Andrew are characters in the story of that call.

We Pray:

For ears to hear the invitation to live fully,
Give us hearts O God, to hear your invitation.
For courage to respond to the invitation to leave our nets,
Give us hearts O God, to hear your invitation.
For faith to follow the invitation to journey's end, we pray,
Give us hearts O God, to hear your invitation.

O love of God in the heart of Jesus, you called us in our Baptism to be the hands and heart of Jesus Christ. May we never fail to answer the invitation to love as Jesus loved and may we sail our boats to the heart of the universe.

An Invitation Prayer:

May you hear the voice of God whispered in the wind, crashing to the shore, and may you follow that voice to the place of discovery.

May you see the mind of God in the seasons of beginnings and endings, in the darkness and light of each day, and may you follow that mind into enlightenment.

May you find the hand of God in the rainbow, sketching the moods of heaven and earth, holding the circle of life, and may you follow that hand in the direction of your destiny.

May you ponder the beauty of God in still waters and in desert spaces, in the meeting of friends and in the question of a child, and may you follow that beauty to its source.

May you feel the presence of God on the strong shoulder that supports your sorrow, in the human teardrop that shares your joy, and may you follow that presence to the mountain top.

May you experience the blessing of God on the journey across the distance, in the walking and climbing, in the ascending and descending, and may that blessing lead you safely home.

May you touch the heart of God in the stone that rolls back, in the robin that flies in winter, in the gift of a rose, and may the heart of God fill your decisions with love.

May you learn the secret of God's love in the heart of Jesus Christ, in his emptying and in his filling, in his receiving and in his giving, and may the Sacred Heart of Jesus teach you how to love.

THE HEART REMEMBERS

Christian charity is first of all the simple response to immediate needs and specific situations.

(*Deus caritas est*, 46)

A WORD OF THANKS:
He threw himself at Jesus' feet and thanked him. (Luke 17:16)

It wasn't just the new skin or the relief from rotting flesh that called me back. I remembered the touch. It was the first one in ten years, as contact with others was forbidden in the leper colony. Even the domestic animals recoiled from the leper's smell and at our approach the sun itself withdrew her warmth. I imagined that death would come like a slow paralysis of feeling; it would be like the loss of human touch, a place of fear and despair.

The day began early for the ten of us. We knew that Jesus was in town so we defied the social barriers and made a run for the man from Galilee. I saw him first! In the same instant he saw me. I retreated back into the shadows of the olive tree, and with my body bent beneath the green foliage I tried to stifle the sound of my breathing. Then he was there beside me, his great arm reaching out a hand to my hand. He held my dying limb and massaged the withered skin. His eyes were filling with tears and I knew that he cried for the ten lepers.

I was standing now, upright, wrapt in the shelter of his strength, released in the dignity of his friendship. Love had touched my body again, after a lifetime of waiting. As the rags of filth and fear fell from my hands that day, I knew that I had seen the face of God. I went back to say thanks. With every footprint I wrote it in the sand; with every breath I spoke it to the wind. When I finally caught up with him he seemed to be expecting me. I said 'thank you' until my voice stopped. The heart remembers the moment.

We Pray:

> For the healing of my heart,
> Thanks be to God.
> For the touch that says 'I love you',
> Thanks be to God.
> For the release from fear and rejection,
> Thanks be to God.

> O love of God in the heart of Jesus, we thank you for loving
> us, for taking away our shame and our fear. Your love is a
> healing touch, restoring our broken spirits. All our trust,
> O God, is in your love. Amen.

A WORD OF WELCOME:
'Do you see this woman? I came into your home and you gave me
no water for my feet, but she has washed my feet with her tears and
dried them with her hair.' (Luke 7:44)

She came with ointment. It was the most expensive that she
could find. She had followed him for many miles observing the
magnificence of his heart. The woman felt herself responding to
the acceptance that poured out from his person, to the wonder
of a heart at work. He opened to her the secrets of her own
compassion. In his presence she was more and his words were a
new horizon on her soul. She who had known the emptiness of
exploitation, longed for someone who would raise her up.

The woman followed him that day to the house of Simon.
He was seated at table with the invited guests. Noticing Simon's
embarrassment by her presence in his house, the woman from
the streets moved quietly to the feet of the teacher. She who had
come to welcome the guest was drawn into the fire of a holy
presence, for he was also welcoming her. Her spirit revived and
her body trembled, and her tears turned to pools of living water.
She washed his feet, removed the sand, then smoothed them
with her hands and dried them with her hair. As she felt the

weight of his fatigue and loneliness, she knew the importance of her hospitality.

Simon hadn't welcomed him, and the woman who had often experienced rejection opened her jar of ointment and let it flow over his skin, into the dried crevices, down to the tips of his toes. She kissed his feet, holding them, healing them, just as she had seen him do. She ignored the whispered judgements and poured out her heart. Wherever this story is told the welcome of one woman is remembered.

We Pray:

When we gather our family and friends,
With all my heart I welcome you, O God.
When we sit down to table,
With all my heart I welcome you, O God.
When other doors are closed before you,
With all my heart I welcome you, O God.

O love of God in the heart of Jesus, you reveal the depths of God. The winds blow with your freedom and the woman cries with your acceptance. All our trust, O God, is in your love. Amen.

A WORD OF PROMISE:
This is my body, which is given for you. Do this in remembrance of me. (Luke 23:19b)

A promise is a word to last for ever. A promise from Jesus who had made flesh the heart of God and carried on his shoulders the weight of broken promises, had the unique quality of an unconditional gift. He was with them in Galilee and they came to understand a man of his word. They experienced how he himself lived in faithful response to the memory of God's redemptive plan for all creation and how he fulfilled his role as prophet to the nations. Especially, they were eyewitnesses of his ability to take away hunger and when he blessed the bread and gave them the promise of his abiding presence, they learned the secret of the ages.

Jesus actualised the memory of God and in doing so became himself the living memory, the dangerous memory of opposition. Jesus was a dangerous memory because he denounced systems of oppression and corruption, questioning the power of Rome. His words and actions matched, and his message was consistent with justice, compassion and peace. When he asked to be remembered in the breaking of the bread, the memory became irrefutable and the promise was secured for all time.

Remembering is the life of the story. It holds its shape when the physical reality is no longer available. It releases the legacy and realises the dream. It is remembering that discovers beginnings at the empty tomb and stories for the road ahead. When we remember, we are keepers of the promise.

We Pray:

For memories that take us beyond the empty tomb,
May we remember what he told us.
For memories that complete the story,
May we remember what he told us.
For memories that connect us to eternity,
May we remember what he told us.

O love of God in the heart of Jesus, we thank you for the gift of your love in the flesh of your son. You are God without beginning or ending and in Jesus you extend a living memory to your people. May we never forget Galilee and his promise to rise again. All our trust, O God, is in your love. Amen.

A REMEMBERING PRAYER:

We bow our heads in solemn remembrance and pray:
You remembered us O God, and our cries reached your ears.
You came down to us and led us out of Egypt. We remember
the hour of release and we sing the prayer of the covenant.

You remembered us O God, and your hand reached
out to restore our flesh. You saw us in the hiding place
where outcasts shelter and you touched us back to life.
We remember the hour of hope and we sing the prayer of
thanksgiving.

You remembered us O God, and your angels sang tidings of
great joy in the night. You trusted the shepherds with the
breaking news of salvation. We remember the hour of the
global exodus and we sing the prayer of wonder.

You remembered us O God, and you welcomed us back from
the prisons of doubt and self-rejection. You waited for our
coming and satisfied our longing. We remember the hour of
acceptance and we sing the prayer of homecoming.

You remembered us O God, and you pleaded our cause in
the courts of the just. On the evidence of love you defended
us and we became a new creation. We remember the hour of
forgiveness and we sing the prayer of new birth.

You remembered us O God, and you gave us Jesus to lead
us to the New Jerusalem. In his dying and in his rising he
has become the living memorial of our redemption. We
remember the hour of victory and we sing the prayer of
Eucharist.

THE HEART FORGIVES

> God's passionate love for his people – for humanity – is at the same time a forgiving love. It is so great that it turns God against himself, his love against his justice.

> (Deus caritas est, 10)

THE LONG ABSENCE:
When his father saw him, his heart was full of pity and he ran,
threw his arms round his son, and kissed him. (Luke 15:20)

I was looking for love. The space inside me was empty and deep and like all empty spaces, it yearned to be filled. I decided to search for my pot of gold and I left my father's house to find a home. My mother, having carefully prepared food for the journey, waved goodbye to her second son.

I was looking for more. My father's money was magic! I partied the nights away and I tasted the cocktails of alcoholic wonder. With money I had an unrestricted passport to oblivion. At first it was a reckless and exciting adventure, but slowly I began to learn that the more I wanted, the less I seemed to have.

I was looking for a release. In silent gutters I had abandoned my senses to external controls, until my very self began to slip away. I wasted the daylight and I squandered the peace of night, but through my tears I remembered the home of my youth, my mother's presence and my father's faithfulness and how they never stopped waiting for me. One day my tears turned to whispers, calling me home.

It was a morning in September when I left the city shelter. My mother who kept watch from the kitchen window took my hand in hers and rubbed it back to life. My father ran from the field, his arms opened wide to hold me again. When he kissed me I knew I was home. As we sat down to bacon, eggs and freshly brewed coffee, I understood why they call God 'Mother' and 'Father.'

We Pray:

> For my absence from the family, I am sorry,
> Lord have mercy.
> For my absence from the community, I am sorry,
> Lord have mercy.
> For my absence from the relationship, I am sorry,
> Lord have mercy.

> O love of God in the heart of Jesus, you desire to bring
> forgiveness and reconciliation to your people. Even when
> we are lost in bad choices and in dark places you wait for us
> and love us back to life. Our trust, O God, is in your love.
> Amen.

THE WRONG CHOICE:
Truly I tell you, today you will be with me in paradise. (Luke 23:43)

The dream of youth had fallen apart for me and one failed choice led to another. With years of disappointment and falling down, I began to fight my lost youth by stealing from others. Shadows of crime and isolation seemed to offer cover and strength, but they encircled me with the illusion of safety and I sank deeper into the night. It had to end, this lost youth, and death would bring escape. I had longed to see the rising sun but it was too late for another chance and I was listed for crucifixion.

There were three of us on death row in this final hour so at least I would not die alone. One was angry and blasphemous but the other one was mysteriously silent. I could read the inscription 'Jesus of Nazareth, King of the Jews' over his cross. This was enough to send any man down! Little did I know that I would share my final hours with the preacher who had caused social, political and religious upheaval in the land. I knew him to be a man without malice and it was said of him that he knew the secrets of the heart in every person.

I looked at him and he was looking at me. His eyes had survived the hatred, and face to face with the thief they glistened with mercy. In that moment of communion I remembered hearing how he once spoke of second chances and of finding lost sheep. I remembered that he had made his home with sinners and with a single touch or word he had given back what was stolen from broken hearts. I believed that my hour had come! 'Remember me!' – the words tumbled from my fading breath but I held on for the chance. Yes! I would be with him in paradise. The dream was saved in the mercy of the cross.

We Pray:

For another chance to seek forgiveness,
Jesus, remember me.
For another day to discover hope,
Jesus, remember me.
For another moment to experience love,
Jesus, remember me.

O love of God in the heart of Jesus, you wait for us in the final hour. Even when all seems lost and the chance is fading, you turn despair to hope. Give us faith, O God, to return to you though our debts be great. Remember us and show us your mercy. Our trust, O God, is in your love. Amen.

THE BLIND FEAR:
Father forgive them for they do not know what they are doing. (Luke 23:34)

As a man lives, so shall he die. The words of forgiveness from the cross give the final signature to the heart of God on earth. It's what we expected at the end of a life of unconditional generosity and love. He, the free man, was utterly forgiving. Forgiveness is always heroic and when whispered from the cross it takes our breath away. We hear it in the courtroom and at the scene of tragedy, in the death of an innocent child and where brother kills brother. It is life's ultimate achievement, the finest hour of the human heart.

Forgiveness is not only a decision of the intellect, it is the victory of choice. It neither recriminates nor measures punishment but simply releases the debtor, for the forgiving person has learned that the cost of hatred is high both physically and emotionally. To forgive is to release oneself from pounds of flesh and settling scores. When we make things right, the peace offering expands the heart of the giver and the receiver. Then, in that place beyond forgiveness, there is love.

Only forgiveness is big enough for God! Only what God has done for us defines forgiveness. From the cross Jesus testified to the very nature of God, not as a victim of injustice but as a brother of humankind. Ours were the sins he bore; ours were the burdens he carried. He was neither diminished nor distorted by memories of our inhumanity for he wanted to forgive and forget the sin. His forgiveness was his gift for the release of all creation.

We Pray:

> For the gift of God's mercy in our relationships,
> Father, forgive us as we forgive others.
> For the comfort of God's mercy in our guilt,
> Father, forgive us as we forgive others.
> For the healing of God's mercy in our memories,
> Father, forgive us as we forgive others.

> O love of God in the heart of Jesus, your mercy brims over with love and your forgiveness outshines the obscenity of violence and hatred. May I never crucify another person by withholding forgiveness and may I be the first to cross the bridge of peace. Our trust, O God, is in your love. Amen.

A FORGIVENESS PRAYER:

I heard your cry of hunger but I passed by on the other side.
Forgive me, my brother, for the times when I abandoned you
to poverty and failed to share my bread.
Forgive us our sins as we forgive others.

I saw your struggle with violence but I passed by on the other
side. Forgive me, my sister, for the times when I ignored your
bruises and remained silent.
Forgive us our sins as we forgive others.

I knew that you were betrayed but I passed by on the other
side. Forgive me, my friend, for the times when I was dishonest
with you and supported the lie.
Forgive us our sins as we forgive others.

I remembered your plea for compassion but I passed by on the
other side. Forgive me, my neighbour, for the times when I
closed the door and ignored your presence.
Forgive us our sins as we forgive others.

I witnessed your pain and sorrow but I passed by on the other
side. Forgive me, my colleague, for the times when I was too
busy to go back for you.
Forgive us our sins as we forgive others.

I said that I would never forgive and never forget and I passed
by on the other side. Forgive me, my people, for the times
when I refused to cancel your debt and set you free.
Forgive us our sins as we forgive others.

THE HEART SERVES

> A Eucharist which does not pass over into the concrete
> practice of love is intrinsically fragmented.

> (*Deus caritas est, 14*)

A WAITING PEOPLE:
*Then Mary said, 'Here I am, the servant of the Lord; let it be with
me according to your word'. (Luke 1:38)*

In the Hebrew Bible the people who cooperate with the plan
of God in faithfulness to the covenant are the servants of God.
Mary of Nazareth joined her voice to the voices of all who believed
in the fulfilment of God's promise. Her offer of service became a
lifeline to resurrection for a waiting people.

The word 'servant' occurs over a thousand times in the Bible
and it implies a willingness to bind oneself to God, in faith and
in action. The title 'God's servant' is one of honour, expressing
a relationship of total engagement. It is through the servants of
God that the story of 'God-with-us' is told and remembered. In
the fullness of time, salvation itself comes to us through the one
who came to serve and to give his life as a ransom for many.
Mary, as God bearer, is in service of salvation for all creation.

Mary will be remembered for all generations because her
role of service links all humanity to its destiny with God. As a
servant of God, Mary's lowly state is transformed and hope flows
for the release of all who are hungry. In Mary, the great plan
of social justice that the prophets spoke about is unveiled. She
stands at a threshold in the biblical story, and the servant of God
is now linking ancient Israel to unending life. This ultimately is
the essential role of God's servant, to refer all reality to God.
Cooperation with God's plan brings release in the now as in the
future.

We Pray:

> In service may we release the best in people,
> Here I am Lord, I come to do your will.
> In service may we direct the world to Jesus Christ,
> Here I am Lord, I come to do your will.
> In service may we open prison doors,
> Here I am Lord, I come to do your will.

> O love of God in the heart of Jesus, we thank you for calling
> us to serve your people. May our service be loving and may
> our loving reveal your justice and peace from age to age. We
> place our trust in your heart, emptied for the life of the world.

A HUNGRY MULTITUDE:
You, yourselves, give them something to eat. (Luke 9:13)

Food has a gathering effect and the promise of food draws
people. Those who have nothing seek relief from physical hunger
and those who have plenty seek relief from too much. The
multitude in the gospel story highlights the issue of hunger as one
of humanity's greatest problems. The thousands who clamoured
for food at the end of the day widen our perspective on the famine
of the heart.

On this particular occasion the demand for food is presented
both as a problem of provision and provider. Food is given, not
taken, and the provider has the responsibility of service. The
apostles were overwhelmed. Hunger does that: it is urgent,
monstrous and embarrassing. Jesus was unreserved in making
relief from hunger the responsibility of his disciples. Even where
resources are extremely limited before a scale of great magnitude,
the cry of hunger must not be ignored. Disciples of Christ are by
definition agents of release from hunger. Hunger is my problem.

As the thousands gather in the quiet of the evening they are
tired from long distances travelled in their search for Jesus. He is
with them in their assembling and he is with them as bread; his

disciples would be the guardians of this truth. It is now their turn to be instruments of God's abundance for a hungry world. The bread of life is not a compact ritual but an action of liberation in a world of famine. Like the disciples in Luke's Gospel we also feel helpless before the enormity of the problem, but in Christ the little bread and the fish that we have become the food of life for all the world.

We Pray:

May there be food on my table when you are hungry,
Lord, that we may share.
May there be friendship at my door when you knock,
Lord, that we may share.
May there be love in my heart when we sit at table,
Lord, that we may share.

O love of God in the heart of Jesus, in your birth the universe story is filled out and a fire of longing burns in every living thing. As hunger rages in our time we turn to you for broken bread. All our trust, O God, is in your abundant love. Amen.

A FRIEND AT TABLE:
He rose from the table, took off his outer garment, and tied a towel round his waist. Then he poured some water into a basin and began to wash the disciples' feet. (John 13:4-5)

I returned to Nazareth, to my own people, the ones who had watched me grow and become a man. They had cared for me as a child and had called me their own. I came back to tell them of liberation and to wash their feet in a living spring. But they rejected my service and I left home that day to search for the outsider.

I met a rich man at the temple. He spoke of gold and silver, and of the splendour of temples and synagogues. I offered him the water to release his burden but he turned his back and walked into the distance. I cried inside for another chance that had passed me by. He had the makings of a great and loyal friend, a generous attitude and a big mind, but I wanted more. I wanted to wash his feet, to connect with his heart. I saw him waver for an instant, but then he was gone.

I saw a young woman in the cornfield. She was humming the song of the mountain lark. She looked deeply into my eyes and I saw the freshness of a youth in her morning time. She wanted to follow the dream. I invited her to my table to feed the people from her fields of gold. She almost said 'yes' but at that moment the heartbeat slowed and she went back to walking.

I waited for Judas in the courtyard. His betrayal had cut me to pieces but I held on to the hope that we would work it out. He was a special friend, vulnerable and unsure, but I knew the depth of his uncertainty. I offered him the water and towel but he was still unable to let himself be loved. He left the table. We parted with a kiss.

We Pray:

I give you my hands, O God, for the washing of feet,
Lord, let me be your servant.
I give you my heart, O God, for the drying of tears,
Lord, let me be your servant.
I give you my life, O God, for the love of your people,
Lord, let me be your servant.

O love of God in the heart of Jesus, you never give up the search for the heart of your people. Help us in the dark moments of life to feel the grace of your service for you are the heart in which we trust. Amen.

A Servant's Prayer:

All you rivers serve God, as you flow from the source of life
until the people drink.
All you open wells serve God, as you fill the empty bucket
until the thirst is ended.
All you surging seas serve God, as you keep the timeless
rhythm until the tides are in.

All you tiny dewdrops serve God, as you awaken the dry
earth until the desert rumbles.
All you rain showers serve God, as you nurture the growing
grasses until the meadow blossoms.
All you flood waters serve God, as you restore the waiting
plains until all creation groans.

All you naval vessels serve God, protecting international
waters until the peace is won.
All you fishing boats serve God, waiting through the
darkness until the fish are caught.
All you passenger ships serve God, crossing the great divide
until you find your destination.

All you birds on the wing serve God, announcing the
seasons of light and darkness until the dawn chorus.
All you beasts of the jungle serve God, trusting the earth to
yield its fruit, until all are fed.
All you innocent lambs serve God, dancing with hope and
promise until you reach the slaughter.

All you brave hearts serve God, holding the world together
until the conflict ends.
All you mothers and fathers serve God, humming the
midnight lullaby until the fear has passed.
All you friends and neighbours serve God, gathering round
the table until the meal is shared.

THE HEART TRIUMPHS

So great is God's love for man that by becoming man he follows him even into death, and so reconciles justice and love.

(Deus caritas est, 10)

BEYOND DEATH:
See how much he loved him. (John 11:35)

Lazarus is dead. There is the sound of mourning everywhere. The entire community has come to the village to honour the memory. I have a confusion of feelings in my heart this morning. I loved Lazarus and we had that special understanding that brothers and sisters sometimes have.

The worst part of these days for me has been the absence of Jesus. I will never forget the first hours after Lazarus died and how I waited until the sun had left the sky, but he didn't come. In my wildest dreams I never thought that he would let us down. He was our closest friend, the one who shared every family secret. The cloud broke for me on the fourth day when his figure filled the distance. All I could think of saying was, 'If you had been here my brother would not have died'.

He assured me that Lazarus would rise again on the last day. The promise of the last day wasn't very helpful and my eyes spilled over again. It was his next sentence, however, that really pinned me to the ground. He said that he himself was the resurrection and that those who believed in him would never die. As I led him to the tomb where Lazarus was buried, I began to think how death intensifies love.

His tears flowed down at the grave of Lazarus. He cried as I had never seen him cry before and I could see that his tears reconnected him to the lost presence. There was a great silence in the crowd. Then quite suddenly his voice broke the stillness: 'Take away the stone,' he said. I was there and I saw it happen. Lazarus walked from his tomb that day. The heart of Jesus had triumphed again.

We Pray:

> May love hold us together in life and in death,
> The one who believes in you will never die.
> May Jesus come to us when we weep at the tomb,
> The one who believes in you will never die.
> May the heart of Jesus call us forth from the grave,
> The one who believes in you will never die.

> O love of God in the heart of Jesus, you open the tombs of
> our darkness and fear, and with your tears you reawaken love
> in us. May our tears mingle with yours as we bring forth love
> on earth. Our trust, O God, is in your love. Amen.

BEYOND PAIN:
*He loves you and you love me and have believed that I came from
God. I did come from the Father and I came into the world; and now
I am leaving the world and going to the Father. (John 16:27-28)*

I died in the springtime of my days before my dreams were
full, and your gentle cry and muffled sob followed me to the
horizon until I let go and passed over into the fullness of light. In
death's hour one is broken to pieces and the other is made whole.

I left the time capsule on that sun-filled day as the dawn opened
and the song of angels greeted me. I could see my rising star as it
moved earthward to rejoice at my coming and to lead me home.

In the whisper of the morning breeze against my skin I passed
into heaven remembering your sorrow. My eyes spilled over with
the intensity of the moment as earth and heaven danced before
me.

You were there at the bridge letting me go for I was drawn by
a terrible desire to touch the source. What I saw before me was
beyond my thoughts, beyond my dreams, and I was taken into the
embrace of God.

I do not want you to fall apart; our love is greater than death. Thank you for your love that let me go; you gave me wings, and with the courage and identity of your faith you let me fly that I might be forever young.

Heaven reminds me of my family home. God looks like you. Do not search for me among the dead. I have returned to the beginning, to your God and to my God.

We Pray:

> When we must let go the dreams of youth,
> Jesus, take us with you to God's house.
> When death comes suddenly and without mercy,
> Jesus, take us with you to God's house.
> When life is over and our work is done,
> Jesus, take us with you to God's house.

> O love of God in the heart of Jesus, you have prepared a home for us where every tear will be wiped away. May our journey lead us to the source of eternal peace. Our trust, O God, is in your love. Amen.

BEYOND TIME:
I will be with you always, to the end of time. (Matthew 28:20)

We waited helplessly for darkness to take its course. You were too tired to speak, too bloodied to see. The mob roared and the blows were a frenzy on your flesh. We wanted more than anything to save our own skin so we did nothing. But you came back! You wanted us to touch you again, to feel the marks of your love, to remember the promise. As we stand beside you on the hill outside of Bethany we know that you will never leave us. Your presence is a promise to last for ever.

We had prepared for our wedding vows with precision and excitement; the big moment brought tears of joy and relief. We dreamed our dreams that day and we took to the road together, shoulder to shoulder, heart to heart. The journey led us through quiet pasture and over stormy seas. We laughed and we cried together and our shared purpose became our strength. You were just thirty-five when you fell from the scaffolding. I waited with you for a breakthrough but it was the end of a dream. We have grown old together, still heart to heart. Presence is a promise to last for ever.

The early scan revealed a boy! We would call him Simon and he would play the organ in church as his father and grandfather had done for over half a century. Our son would be a natural progression, a keeper of the name, a link in the chain. His first cry was loud and strong, but his words never came. We believed in Simon, in the person struggling to be freed and we waited with him. The breakthrough came on his fifteenth birthday when he blew his first notes on the old tin whistle. Simon had broken into our world with 'Happy Birthday to You'. Presence is a promise to last for ever.

We Pray:

O God, Give us enough love to carry the cross,
May our love endure for ever.
O God, Give us enough love to survive the pain of loss,
May our love endure for ever.
O God, Give us enough love to persevere in hoping,
May our love endure for ever.

O love of God in the heart of Jesus, you have joined the family line and you have taken us to your heart. Though the mountains fall to the sea we have no fear. Your love is for ever and our trust, O God, is in your love. Amen.

A Victory Prayer:

You lived your life in service, covering extra miles for others and you were there to the finish line. Yours is the generosity and yours is the victory. May God come to meet you with the trophy of service.

You lost your life in the service of peace, leaving family and homeland for the cause of a just world order. Yours is the courage and yours is the victory. May God come to meet you with the trophy of peace.

You kept watch with the heart of a carer, for weeks that became years, and you stayed beyond the sunset. Yours is the faithfulness and yours is the victory. May God come to meet you with the trophy of life.

You waited through the seasons of darkness and light, grappling with depression, believing in days without shadows. Yours is the endurance and yours is the victory. May God come to meet you with the trophy of light.

You rested in the earth for the winter months, trusting the darkness of silence, confident in the song of spring. Yours is the hope and yours is the victory. May God come to meet you with the trophy of new beginnings.

You fought the system through years of frustration and rejection until you won the right to see and know your children. Yours is the heroism and yours is the victory. May God come to meet you with the trophy of justice.

You reared your family with tenderness and care, in plentiful times and in scarce times, always loving, always there. Yours is the dedication and yours is the victory. May God come to meet you with the trophy of the heart.

THE HEART SETS FREE

Love is free; it is not practised as a way of achieving other ends.

(*Deus caritas est*, 31c)

THE LOST SHEEP:
Rejoice with me for I have found my sheep that was lost. (Luke 15:6b)

I am the Good Shepherd. I have played a pivotal role in every civilisation. I understand my sheep, each one of them. They are prey animals, vulnerable and afraid. When they pull away from me the knot tightens on their loneliness and predators wait in the shadows to devour them. Sometimes in their desire for freedom they are easily deceived. I have come with my staff to expose every danger and to let them go free.

I am the Good Shepherd. The sheep that belong to me have a flocking instinct and tend to follow the one that moves first. Without their friends and neighbours they become stressed and afraid, and greedy leaders can exploit them and drive them to desert land. With little defence they tend to scatter in fear. I have come with my staff to keep the sheep together and to let them go free.

I am the Good Shepherd. After all these years the sheep know my voice and they trust the one who remembers their names. At the dawn of each day I call them to green pastures and in the evening they lie down at my counting. Some of my sheep become trapped under the pressure of life but I have come with my staff to open the traps and to let them go free.

I am the Good Shepherd. The care of the flock is my life and I remain with them through every season. I know the hillsides and the cliff face. The map has many landscapes and the road has many turns. I am there at every boulder, at the edge and on the bridge. When the fog falls on their fields they are not afraid of wolves. I have come with my staff to direct them to the safety of the sheepfold and to let them go free.

We Pray:

> The Lord is my Shepherd, I am safe from harm,
> The Lord is my Shepherd, I am not afraid.
> The Lord is my Shepherd, he will come and find me,
> The Lord is my Shepherd, I am not afraid.
> The Lord is my Shepherd, he will bring me safely home,
> The Lord is my Shepherd, I am not afraid.

> O love of God in the heart of Jesus, the sheep come back to you and the lambs lie down with you. You are shepherd and you are home for the flock. We place all our trust, O God, in your love. Amen.

THE HIDDEN GIFT:
The kingdom of heaven is near. Heal the sick, bring the dead back to life, cleanse the lepers and drive out demons. You received this as gift, so give it as gift. (Matthew 10:7-8)

Jane and Adrian were a perfect match. They shared a passion for art and art galleries, and their shared interest took them all over the world in search of the masters. It was the work of Zhao Kailin and his painting of an orphaned child that led the young couple to visit a local orphanage where they came face to face with gifts not yet revealed.

The orphanage that day was airless, with the noise of tears and the cries of the abandoned. Some of the children rocked the time away, others pleaded for possibility. It was Lin Yin who first made a move in Jane's direction. At four years old she was alert in mind but limited in mobility. The tumour on her neck was large, ugly and untreated. As she tugged at Jane's sandal Jane heard the tiny command, 'Lift me up'.

As the woman and the child came face to face they knew that each had a gift to offer the other. It was the possibility of becoming. Later in their hotel, Adrian and Jane discussed the points of contact between art and life. They spoke of Kailin's orphaned child and the gift it was to the human perspective. Would they love her? Would they who had received as gift, give as gift? If they lifted up this one child their lives would be changed for ever.

Lin Yin soon developed an Irish accent and at seventeen she walked the Dublin City Marathon. When she graduated from Art School in 1996, Jane and Adrian encouraged her to walk again in the land of her birth, in its palaces, temples and art galleries that she too might discover possibility.

We Pray:

With the gift of my hands may I relieve pain,
All that I have I offer now to you.
With the gift of my mind may I create beauty,
All that I have I offer now to you.
With the gift of my heart may I love deeply,
All that I have I offer now to you.

O love of God in the heart of Jesus, you are the gift of life at the heart of the universe. You gave your own life to raise us up. Help us to be the gift of your love to others. In your love, O God, we place our trust. Amen.

THE LOWLY SERVANT:
God has remembered the lowly servant. And all generations call her blessed. (Luke 1:48)

The rock was fixed, strong and enduring; the pebble was small and drifted down the river. As a pebble it could go where rocks could not go, and when the rock finally broke the pebble would hold together.

The pebble believed in people who couldn't scale the mountain face and conquer the climb. It believed in shelter for insects and in ripples on the river. As a pebble it was now the cornerstone. It could break the smoothness of the surface current and change the direction of the wave. Although light in weight and irregular in shape, the pebble could open a hole in the ice cap and start a crack in the frozen layer. More importantly, unlike the rocks, one pebble could easily join together with other pebbles to become a purifying system for all who searched for living water.

Over the years the pebble came to experience extraordinary things. It became part of nature's journey, rising, falling, giving, receiving, living, dying. In time it learned that holding on to the ancient rock was a safer option but then it would have missed being part of the new temple. Freed from the rock, the pebble discovered how to become a foundation stone, and while the rocks held on to their power, the pebble sang a Magnificat of liberation.

One day there was a rumbling beneath the earth and the rocks split open and the graves rose up and the only thing left standing was a tree on the hill. When the people saw how the wood stretched out its great arms in the storm they sought shelter beneath the tree. In the morning the rocks had been reduced to pebbles and people spoke of a new world order.

We Pray:

Help us O God to release the gifts in others,
God has visited us and set us free.
Help us O God to lift up the downtrodden,
God has visited us and set us free.
Help us O God to open the snare and free the sheep,
God has visited us and set us free.

O love of God in the heart of Jesus, you bring a new standard to our measurements and in your love the lowly go free. May we never hold values that diminish the heart of humanity. All our trust is in your love. Amen.

A Captive's Prayer:

My heart is silent, my eyes are spent. Fear holds me captive
in its endless whisper of woes. I have learned to move
in chains from my first toddling steps and with time and
practise I have become a captive of tomorrow's fear. O God,
I yearn to come home. Breathe a word of release into the
secret of my heart, unlock my chains and walk with me into
freedom.

My dream is faded and my words are slurred. Substance
abuse has soured my desire for life. From that first moment
when my heart shattered to pieces, I have learned to exist in
fogs of emptiness and loneliness, and I have become a captive
of escape. O God, I yearn to come home. Breathe a word of
awareness into the secret of my heart, unlock my chains and
walk with me into freedom.

My name is blotted out and my chance is gone. Money has
lied to me and reduced my plans to the vacuum of a prison
cell. What started with an honest desire to cross the ghetto
boundary became a thirst for power and control and I
became a captive of greed. O God, I yearn to come home.
Breathe a word of acceptance into the secret of my heart,
unlock my chains and walk with me into freedom.

My life is eroded and my spirit is suppressed. The memory of
violence and violation is distant now but the decision to live
in the memory still controls my path. The theft of my youth
and its freshness has shut out the day and I have become a
captive to the memory. Breathe a word of forgiveness into the
secret of my heart, unlock my chains and walk with me into
freedom.

THE HEART TRUSTS

The universe in which we live has its source in God and was created by him.

(Deus caritas est, 9)

LOOK AT THE RAVENS:
Remember the lilies. Consider the ravens: they neither sow nor
reap, they have neither storehouse nor barn and yet God feeds
them. (Luke 12:24)

The raindrops waited for the cloud to let them go in free fall
down to earth. At first they rested lightly on the silent meadow
but they worried about the sun and if it would return to melt away
the winter seal. A snowdrop on its way to infinity recalled the
ravens and the lilies; the raindrops remembered and they went
on waiting.

The daffodils and primroses were still deep in sleep when the
raindrops crept into their chamber bringing soft drink to greet
their awakening. The first yawns of the stirring seeds were fragile
with little life, but the raindrops, who had remembered the ravens
and the lilies, went on waiting.

The journey into the sunlight was hazardous for the growing
seeds as insects sought sustenance from the tender morsels. A war
of survival was waged beneath the molecules of earth and other
raindrops came to help in the struggle of rebirth. Together they
remembered the ravens and the lilies, and they all waited.

The new buds came out one by one but some hadn't yet
heard about the ravens; the lilies were afraid of the raindrops
and remained folded and closed. The people thought that the
reawakening was too slow and they worried about the harvest, but
the raindrops who remembered the ravens and the lilies waited.

The fear of a late year was eased with the return of cherry
blossoms and the delight of warm days. But one day the sun
began to lower her beams and the people began to worry about

dark evenings and shortage of food. The raindrops, however, remembered that he had said, 'Do not be afraid!' They knew about trust and they waited.

We Pray:

> For release from the bondage of anxiety,
> O God, may we go free.
> For wisdom to learn from the freedom of the birds,
> O God, may we go free.
> For trust in the heart of God,
> O God, may we go free.

> O love of God in the heart of Jesus, help us to unravel the strings of worry and anxiety that kill the life in us and give us the trust of the ravens that we may go free. O Sacred Heart of Jesus we place our trust in you.

OBSERVE THE GROWING SEED:
Whether he is asleep or awake, be it day or night, the seed sprouts and grows he knows not how. (Mark 4:27)

The growing seed teaches us about trust. The digging and planting belong to us but God gives the fruitfulness. Trust is mutual cooperation in a common purpose, a knowledge that each of the partners will be faithful to the cause. Trust is able to rest from labour and to sleep at night because God will watch over the growing seed.

The Parable of the Growing Seed encourages us to keep faithful to planting and, despite the apparent resistance of the soil, to continue to sow the life-giving word in the village shop, at the family table, on the rocks and in the valleys. It is not ours to manage the mystery of life and death but it is ours to believe in the harvest and to trust the God of the cornfield.

Just as there is a planting time there is also a receiving time, a time of hearing and a time of holding. The soil that is frozen in winter is thawed in springtime and hence the importance of not missing the planting season. Seasons vary for each person but for all there is a continuous becoming, and the planting, weeding and watering that we experience in the morning of life are the moments that shape the harvest.

The growing seed needs time and space to wait and to develop. It needs enough water, but not too much, enough sunshine but not too much, enough direction but not too much. It does not submit to rushed maturity, nor to forced expectations for it can only grow where it has time to change. During the growing time we can sleep secure, for God knows the pace of the seed.

We Pray:

In the morning of life may we plant seeds of trust,
I trust in God, I will not be afraid.
In the high noon of life may we water fields of bread,
I trust in God, I will not be afraid.
In the evening of life may we gather at the banquet,
I trust in God, I will not be afraid.

O love of God in the heart of Jesus, you have waited for
us from the beginning, and when our haste and busyness
destroys the balance you wait for us and heal us in your love.
Show us, O God, the wisdom of the growing seed and free
us from the anxiety of a rushed life. Our trust, O God, is in
your love. Amen.

LEARN FROM THE GRAIN OF WHEAT:
Unless a grain of wheat falls to the earth and dies, it remains alone;
but if it dies it produces much fruit. (Mark 12:24)

You had just celebrated your fourth birthday when you developed a rare degenerative condition with a prognosis of imminent death. In an evil and uncompromising way, the illness would cut you off piece by piece before you had time to write your name. We stopped laughing that day with the weight of unbearable sorrow and uncontrollable anger. We decided to fight back.

It was an all-consuming task. We put our lives on hold as we visited libraries and conferred with experts. Other parents with similar stories came forward and joined the team and slowly we began to put the pieces together and to extract the life-saving fluid from a unique chemical composition. The medical world was amazed as the results unfolded. The condition could now be contained and even cured. Alas! It was too late for our son and he died with the departure of the swallows.

Life as we had known and loved it was gone, but we did have options: to allow the memories live, to let the dream develop, to give the heart a chance. Six months after his burial there were new shoots everywhere. We spoke publicly about the disease and the people who walked in darkness saw a light from the grave. I had always known about memories and how they take on a life of their own, something like a grain of wheat.

He gave up his life for someone else, our little boy, just as Jesus had done and others after him. Because they died others began to live and because they live we are all connected to a life without ending.

We Pray:

> For strength in our letting-go times,
> You are the resurrection and the life.
> For generosity in our giving times,
> You are the resurrection and the life.
> For acceptance in our dying times,
> You are the resurrection and the life.

> O love of God in the heart of Jesus, help us to understand that death is discovery and grains that give themselves for grinding become bread for the world. O Sacred Heart of Jesus we place our trust in you. Amen.

A Trust Prayer:

When the road is blocked and I must take another direction,
I place my trust in you.

When the road is long and I must withdraw from the race,
I place my trust in you.

When the road is unclear and I must follow the wild geese
into unknown space, I place my trust in you.

When the road is uneven and I am stuck in the potholes,
I place my trust in you.

When the road is lonely and I must seek companionship
with the shadows, I place my trust in you.

When the road is noisy and I need to withdraw to a quiet
place, I place my trust in you.

When the road is sloping and I am unable to hold on,
I place my trust in you.

When the road is steep and I must turn back, I place my
trust in you.

When the road is tragic and I must say goodbye to the
friends of my youth, I place my trust in you.

When the road is silent and I must walk alone, I place my
trust in you.

When the road is narrow and I must make a life choice,
I place my trust in you.

When the road is ended and I must return home, I place my
trust in you.

THE HEART LISTENS

Love is the light – and in the end, the only light – that can always illuminate a world grown dim and give us the courage needed to keep living and working.

(Deus caritas est, 39)

To the other side:
Jesus bent down and started writing on the ground with his finger.
And as they continued to ask him, he straightened up and said to
them, 'Let anyone among you who has no sin be the first to throw a
stone at her'. (John 8:6-7)

With these searching words, Jesus put a light on the other side
of every story. Face to face with the momentum of hearsay and
the heave of public opinion he closed his heart on stone throwing.
It was a critical verdict-moment in his ministry, a question on all
judgements and all sentences, and he wrote it in the sand.

The exposure of the woman caught in adultery filled the
countryside with fear. Whispers multiplied and the woman was
folded in shame when the keepers of the Law led her before Jesus.
With his knowledge of both sides of the story, Jesus went for the
context and the credentials of the accusers and he wrote the truth
in the sand.

The news of Danny's departure from the family home shocked
the neighbourhood. There was dismay that a man of Danny's
character could 'walk out' on his wife, Monica, and their three
young children. Danny trembled at the thought of losing his
children. The judge, however, remembered the woman in the
gospel and having heard both sides of the story he wrote a fair
verdict in the sand.

Sarah was abandoned in an orphanage at the age of three.
The experience silenced the song of her heart and when she
reconnected with her mother as a young adult, Sarah was
extremely angry. Her mother helped Sarah to revisit the facts,
to hear the other side and to forgive the betrayal. When Sarah

remembered the woman in Galilee she herself recalled stories that were never heard in popular debate and she began to write them in the sand.

We Pray:

> When the story is bad may I be compassionate,
> O God, open our ears to the other side.
> When the story is popular, may I be fair,
> O God, open our ears to the other side.
> When the story is condemning, may I be brave,
> O God, open our ears to the other side.

> O love of God in the heart of Jesus, you know the secret of the heart and you hear the other side of every story. Give us a sense of fairness in our telling of the story. Our trust, O God, is in your love. Amen.

To the silence:

'Lord save us! We are lost!' But Jesus answered, 'Why are you so afraid, you of little faith?' Then he ordered the wind and sea and it became completely calm. The people were astonished and said, 'What kind of man is he?' (Matthew 8:25-27)

It was the morning of Christmas Day 2009, when the fire lit up the road to Bethlehem. The angels were silent as the great roof of Saint Mel's Cathedral, Longford, that had sheltered the prayers of thousands, fell to the ground and embers of sacred memories littered the town square. The news from Bethlehem deepened the listening time and the great dome was visible above the smoke.

The standing-still in the frozen air brought the community more closely together to whisper words of disbelief and to scan the skyline for a star. On Christmas morning flames of fire were already shaping a new perspective and the heavens embraced the fragments of a faith history that told the good news to all the people.

As the people made their way to Bethlehem their silence was deep with the candlelight of prayer. They remembered famine and war, destruction and death, and the faith that would not be silenced. They remembered their ancestors who built the great cathedral, and they promised on Christmas Day 2009 to be a living cathedral for their children and their children's children.

When the storm died the memorial to the great fire was the people. When the rubble came to rest in the local dump the people still gathered to worship and to open a new chapter in their covenant story. They who had stood together in the silence of the storm went on to Bethlehem to find the child. What kind of people are these?

We Pray:

When our best plans perish,
Help us O Lord, to stand together.
When we have to let go of our dreams,
Help us O Lord, to stand together.
When the things we cherish fall to pieces,
Help us O Lord, to stand together.

O love of God in the heart of Jesus, you stand still for us in the storms of life. Heal the fear and anxiety that threaten us and help us believe in the fire. Our trust, O God, is in your love. Amen.

To the question:
*'Some say that you are John the Baptist; others say that you are
Elijah ...' Again Jesus asked them, 'Who then do you say I am?'
(Luke 9:19-20)*

Who do you say I am? I was with God in the beginning when the empty space began to fill and the great lights opened the heavens. I offered myself in the beginning to mark the map of history with the blood of the covenant. The fields and the oceans began to breathe and all creation took up the groan of new birth. It was the longing of God's love that linked my life to yours in the soil of the earth. The great awakening filled creation with a hunger beyond all telling and I offered myself as bread for the world. Who do you say that I am?

The prophets and prophetesses saw the signs of the time and their cries went out to all the world directing the people to the rising sun. I was born of a woman to reveal the heart of God to all who hunger and thirst. In this time as human talent becomes aware of its increasing capacity, who do you say I am?

It was my desire in the beginning to be the signpost on your journey, giving you wisdom for yielding and awareness on your right-of-way. I was there at every crossroads guiding the lost and picking up the stray. As the globalisation of networks now offers new prophets and new directions, who do you say I am?

Tell John that it is now decision time! I became one with the people in their hunger and darkness, that they might go free. I opened their systems to irrigation and I stripped their laws of oppression. I released from blindness and from bondage that all hearts might taste the breath of God. With a river of mercy I set creation free. Who do you say I am?

We Pray:

> When I see the wonder of the universe, I proclaim,
> You are the Christ, the Son of God.
> When I hear the voices of creation, I proclaim,
> You are the Christ, the Son of God.
> When I experience generosity and mercy, I proclaim,
> You are the Christ, the Son of God.

> O love of God in the heart of Jesus, in your birth you became
> a question for the nations and in the story of the universe you
> are the depth in the mystery. May we see in your heart the
> heart of God. Our trust, O God, is in your love. Amen.

A Listening Prayer:

Dear God,

Let me hear the breaking ice in January that I may release my frozen heart.

Let me hear the silent snowdrop in February that I may believe the impossible.

Let me hear the poem of the daffodils in March that I may dance in the fields.

Let me hear the bleating of the lambs in April that I may understand sacrifice.

Let me hear the cuckoo song in May that I may stand still.

Let me hear the laughter of children in June that I may be eternally young.

Let me hear the holidaymakers in July that I may appreciate resting times.

Let me hear the Song of Mary in August that I may be safe from harm.

Let me hear the game birds in September that I may be food for the hungry.

Let me hear the tales of ghosts in October that I may ponder mystery.

Let me hear the howling wind in November that I may remember those who have passed over.

Let me hear the Christmas bells in December that I may go over to Bethlehem.

THE HEART SURVIVES DEATH

> *Jesus portrays his own path, which leads through to the Cross and Resurrection: the path of the grain of wheat that falls to the ground and dies, and in this way bears much fruit.*
>
> (*Deus caritas est,* 6)

IN THE FAITH OF MARTHA:
Did I not tell you that if you believed you would see the glory of God? (John 11:40)

The young mother was dying. Her nine-year-old son, Timbani, had pushed the wheelbarrow for ten kilometres to get his mother to the bush hospital. He held the plastic bottle of intravenous fluid all through the night, first in his arms, then in his teeth. His mother died as the sun rose over the Zambezi River. The nurse wheeled the woman's body back to the village, for in death she too had seen the glory of God.

The young child was unable to blow out the candles on his birthday cake. The doctor said that Seán Óg was tubercular and he warned the family to avoid direct contact with the child. On the night before his fourth birthday, as Seán Óg began to lose his battle for life, his father gently lowered his mouth to the mouth of his child and gave him the breath of his own breath. At the funeral service the doctor told the people that in the death of this child he too had seen the glory of God.

The mother and father had begged for a house of their own. Their seven children were constantly sick from the conditions on the campsite and they had been standing in the queue for twenty years. On 4 October, the news came that Mary McGuire had died and had left her house and garden to the young family. They had never met Mary McGuire in life but in her death they too saw the glory of God.

The guards arrived at 2 a.m. and the father read the news in their eyes. His beautiful daughter of eighteen years was dead. The journey to James Connolly Memorial Hospital was shrouded in grief. When they saw her lifeless body, still beautiful, her parents knew that in her death she would reveal the glory of God. They donated her organs to someone else.

We Pray:

> Help us O God to see your face in the dark times,
> You are the resurrection and the life.
> Help us O God to hear your voice in the silent times,
> You are the resurrection and the life.
> Help us O God to feel your heart in the death times,
> You are the resurrection and the life.
>
> O love of God in the heart of Jesus, stay close to us in our
> times of grief and pain. May our faith hold together when our
> hearts are broken. O Sacred Heart of Jesus we place our trust
> in you.

IN THE DESERT:
Jesus was led by the Spirit into the wilderness to be tempted by the devil. He fasted for forty days and forty nights, and afterwards he was famished. (Matthew 4:1-2)

The image of the desert is frequently used to express the experience of desolation: those times in our lives that are akin to death itself. It is a moment that sinks us deeply into our capacity and desire for survival. When hunger and thirst, incompleteness and barrenness famish the body, the spirit expands in its longing for God and in its power over endings. Somehow, when the life is drained from us in the emotional endings of our lives, we discover new beginnings where the light is deeper and where the desert is still with mystery.

Historically in the story of ancient Israel and in Christian spirituality, the desert has always been a place where people went to find God. In the place of absence they found presence; in the place of silence they heard whispering sands until death and dying began to tremble with life. With manna from heaven and water from the rock, the desert revealed its secret. The awakening, however, was fraught with struggle and with turning back, for Israel, like ourselves, bowed to another god to escape the birthing time.

Jesus was led by the Spirit into the desert to confront the power of evil. Alone with the agent of death and starved of food and drink he struggled with dispossession and wrestled with the temptation to give in to death in its various guises. In this place devoid of confusion Jesus was filled with the clarity of his mission. The triumph of the desert for all of us was Jesus' return to Galilee, to give his life for the people and to end death for ever. The heart survives the desert.

We Pray:

> When life is empty and we have to walk alone,
> Be close to us O Lord until the morning comes.
> When part of us dies in the long goodbye,
> Be close to us O Lord until the morning comes.
> When we are tempted to give up on life,
> Be close to us O Lord until the morning comes.

> O love of God in the heart of Jesus, sustain us in our desert times, fill the emptiness of our dying space and lead us to the desert well where hearts find water to beat again. All our trust, O God, is in your love. Amen.

IN MEMORY OF THE WOMEN:
Remember how he told you while he was still in Galilee that the Son of Man must be handed over to sinners and be crucified, and on the third day rise again. (Luke 24:6-8)

As we join Mary Magdalene and the other women at the dawning of another day, they are on their way to the tomb. Very few words are exchanged in this atmosphere of bewilderment and concern about the task in hand; together we quicken our steps. The one for whom we risked so much, who attracted our love and loyalty, has died a dishonourable death. The shame of it is beginning to grip the land. Some are even talking about a fake messiah, the one who cheated on his friends. At this moment, however, we are remembering the one who raised us up.

Many of his disciples couldn't take the humiliation and they fled, with apology. Somehow we were unable to forget and so we began the journey back to the tomb, to reopen the story, to revisit the case, to reassess the evidence, to give every man his due anointing. 'Who will role the stone away?' Mary whispered. With Mary you never knew whether she was talking about real stones or the heavier ones of prejudice, intimidation and public opinion. We knew that alone we were powerless to split the block of cultural powers and reveal the identity of the man on the cross. However, despite the obvious problem of access to the truth we moved quietly but resolutely into the dawn. Somehow we would get behind the stone.

The garden was silent and the morning lights revealed the treetops and the burial places. It was Salome who first noticed the opening in the rock. Forgiveness had cut through the great divide and life had defeated death for ever. As we ran back into the hills with the news, the birds and the grasses, the rivers and the sands took up the chorus. The heart had triumphed over death.

We Pray:

When we are condemned for the guilty,
Risen Jesus, lead us beyond death into life.
When we are separated from family and friends,
Risen Jesus, lead us beyond death into life.
When the stone of rejection silences our story,
Risen Jesus, lead us beyond death into life.

O love of God in the heart of Jesus, open the doors of our
hearts to the people we have locked out. Push away the
stones that separate us from forgiveness and truth. All our
trust is in your love. Amen.

AN EASTER PRAYER:

At the dawning of the day, we pray for the blessing of rebirth that new frontiers may be opened in every human heart. May our thinking be expanded and our awareness deepened as the night gives way to day.

In the morning of this day, we pray for the blessing of surprise that we may stand with hope in the empty space and feel the changed presence. In faithfulness to the memory may we roll back the stones of separation and uncover the passage behind every rock.

In the noon of this day, we pray for the blessing of good news that we may hear a new song and know a joy beyond all telling. As sunlight moves across the night of silence may we feel the glory of firelight in our hearts.

In the evening of this day we pray for the blessing of recognition that we may come to know the heart of this Easter day, its memory and its promise. As the stillness settles and the people gather for the meal, may our hearts burn with gratitude in the closeness of this friend.

At the ending of this day we pray for the blessing of gratitude that we may hold the victory of Easter in the secret of our hearts. As the stone is rolled away may we arise from our tombs of shame and discouragement, of uncertainty and confusion and may we change the system that buried a good and innocent man.

THE HEART ACTS JUSTLY

Within the community of believers there can never be room for a poverty that denies anyone what is needed for a dignified life.

(Deus caritas est, 20)

TELL JOHN:
*Go and tell John what you have seen and heard: the blind receive
their sight, the lame walk, the lepers are cleansed ... (Luke 7:22)*

We all look for signs and make signs. God also gives signs.
Signs are fingerprints, evidence that we passed through, our
presence in time and place. The earth is marked with signs of
the search and discovery of people in prayer times, in changing
times, in war times, in peace times, in tragic times, in celebration
times. Signs remind all generations of both the possibilities and
distortions of love. They are keepers of the story, memories of the
struggle.

When John's disciples came in search of proof of Jesus'
identity, Jesus pointed them to the signs he was leaving on the
landscape of Galilee. Everywhere people were living again and
freedom was once more the defining evidence of a divine plan
in progress. A healing hand of love was reaching out to touch
eyes that were blind and ears that were closed. Compassion was
the sign. It was opening new frontiers in words, attitudes and
relationships. Perceptions began to change and cultural creeds
began to tremble. Reality itself was up for questioning and a new
order was entering our language.

The sign was like nothing we had seen before. It slowed the
airbus to a halt and put speed limits on the front runners. It
pointed the rich people to the feeding station and it directed the
poor people to wells of living water. The words on the sign were
written in the language of the learner: the blind see, the deaf hear;
those in bondage are set free.

We Pray:

> For compassion to reach into the heart of life,
> O God, may our sign be compassion.
> For compassion to ease pain and melt obstacles,
> O God, may our sign be compassion.
> For compassion to change systems with forgiveness,
> O God, may our sign be compassion.
>
> O love of God in the heart of Jesus, you have revealed to
> us the sign of compassion, pointing us in new directions,
> to places where people are locked in. May our hearts be
> instruments of release on the earth and may our sign be
> compassion. O Sacred Heart of Jesus, we place our trust in
> you.

TELL MY BROTHERS:
*My son, remember that in your lifetime you were well off while the
lot of Lazarus was misfortune. (Luke 16:25)*

I am a rich man and without apology. My money was hard
earned and carefully managed. I did no harm and I have no
debts, so do not lay the guilt of the nation at my door. I know
about Lazarus and the world is full of them. He is at my gate
day and night but he never bothers to look my way and to be
honest, I have no desire to get involved. It's time for him to do
something for himself. The proximity of this kind of poverty
is best ignored in a neighbourhood like ours. Unfortunately he
seems to be attracting the dogs, something I dislike intensely, so
it's high time for the authorities to clean up the mess.

I am Lazarus and I have come to the rich man's gate. I think
he's afraid to be seen talking to me. He has his own kind of
poverty, I suppose, and he's really very isolated. At least I get
to listen to the birds and talk to the dogs. I do understand that
he has a reputation to safeguard but I'm only looking for a few
scraps, the kind that gets thrown out anyway.

The rich man had his passport to life withdrawn. Even his family connection to Abraham was inadequate for the processing requirements. Lazarus, however, with empty pockets and a stray dog in his arms, seemed to walk in unhindered. The rich man had then called out to Lazarus and even said his name but the distance between them was too great. 'Please go and warn my brothers about the sin of "I don't care",' he pleaded, but Abraham assured the rich man that his brothers had the Scriptures to guide them.

We Pray:

> Lord, that I may see the person who sits at my gate,
> Open my heart, Lord.
> Lord, that I may hear the silence of the hungry heart,
> Open my heart, Lord.
> Lord, that I may welcome Lazarus to my table,
> Open my heart, Lord.

> O love of God in the heart of Jesus, give us new hearts and new minds that we may act justly, love tenderly and walk humbly with all creation. We make our prayer through Jesus, in whose love we place our trust. Amen.

TELL THE TENANTS:
So it will be: the last will be first, the first will be last. (Matthew 20:16)

The Parable of the Tenants has a way of making us uncomfortable. We had a different idea of justice, the kind that is mathematical and fits concisely into our computer programmes. We wanted justice to be according to productivity and profile, and personality and sponsorship, and we had learned to live comfortably with a system where your work is valued in millions, while mine is valued in units. The problem with our calculations, however, is their failure to level the playing field, to acknowledge handicaps and to identify the situations that give peace to some, while bringing others to their knees.

The Parable of the Tenants is an eye-opener. Our justice equation does not add up. The Kingdom of God will not submit to exclusion; it will remain open until the last weary traveller comes to rest. The silver coin is available to anyone who makes it to the vineyard, even at the eleventh hour. To have persevered on the journey, surviving the open road, accepting rejections, walking barefooted, is enough reference material for a job in the vineyard. Eleventh hour justice is the salary of equality.

The Parable of the Tenants has a particular challenge in this time of economic struggle. As competition intensifies and markets crumble we are sensitised once more to the people for whom the vineyard is an elusive dream. Many people have chosen to ask for less so that others may ask for something. Life's marathon is about finishing the course, even at the eleventh hour. In times of economic hardship, we learn the importance of tenants who share the vineyard.

We Pray:

When we come home at the eleventh hour,
Lord, take us into the vineyard.
When we have run out of options,
Lord, take us into the vineyard.
When our best efforts fail,
Lord, take us into the vineyard.

O love of God in the heart of Jesus, be patient with my slow pace, forgive my lack of purpose and spare me a silver coin when I am in financial need. All my trust is in your love. Amen.

A JUSTICE PRAYER:

Give us, O God, a heart where peace and justice make their home. May we see in every day an opportunity for release from oppression.

In the decisions of our lives, help us to protect those who are vulnerable. May we be resolute in guarding against exploitation and privileges that cause suffering.

In the race for banking privileges, may we expose corruption and speak courageously on behalf of the people who beg for bread.

When famine invades the earth and innocent people pay the debt of the guilty, may no one go hungry because of our abundance. Help us, O God, to remember to leave grapes in our fields for the stranger.

When war divides families and nations, we pray that we may be peacemakers and peacekeepers. May we always take the side of forgiveness so that the oppressed and the oppressor may go free.

When people cry freedom, may we raise men and women who are neither anointed by Roman scholarship nor earmarked by existing powers. Bring forth for us, O God, leaders who will release the heart of Church and State.

Give us, O God, a deep sense of the magnificence of life on the changing continents. May our understanding of justice call us into the sacred space of earth and may we be responsible citizens in the web of life.

At this time in history, when the movement of peoples offers a meeting place for races and cultures, teach us, O God, the wonder of diversity and the possibility of a world at peace.

Come to us, O God. Come into our time, stunning in achievement, shaken in failure. Come to our faith that we may stand the test of change. May we hold all people justly, in the secret of our hearts.

THE HEART IS NEIGHBOUR

Anyone who needs me, and whom I can help, is my neighbour. The concept of 'neighbour' is now universalised, yet it remains concrete.

(*Deus caritas est, 15*)

ON THE STREET:
He went to him and bandaged his wounds, having poured oil and wine on them. Then he put him on his own animal, brought him to an inn and took care of him. (Luke 10:34)

I saw you on the street that day as I passed on the other side. You were bloodied and badly beaten, but in an age of mobile phones I was sure that someone else would call an ambulance. Besides, these city streets are dangerous and people who get involved in helping sometimes get accused themselves. One cannot be too careful so I let common sense decide and passed on by.

I thought of the priest and the Levite as I waited at the bus stop, and of how they had to act cautiously lest they became ritually unclean. Failure in mercy can so often be a case of self-protection and sometimes we are blinkered and imprisoned by the laws that we guard with care. On the other side of the road I was in the safety of the Law but I did crave the magnificence of the new temple.

I wondered, as I passed by that day, about the system that allowed thieves and robbers to prosper. Protecting people against thugs was surely the business of the authorities. One should not collude with a faltering system by doing the job of the ones who get paid. This was common sense so I had every reason to pass by.

I did think of the Samaritan himself as I neared my destination. He was the free one in the story, unfettered by temple scholarship and the tenets of the Law. He was free to feel and to bend down and to put his credit card on the line for the stranger on the road. Most of all he was free to think outside the system and to be a neighbour.

We Pray:

> May we be safe from harm on our journey through life,
> Protect us O God and keep us safe.
> May we have friends to support us in difficult times,
> Protect us O God and keep us safe.
> May we be good neighbours wherever we live,
> Protect us O God and keep us safe.

> O love of God in the heart of Jesus, you took the risk of emptying yourself and you bent down to pick us up when we were lost in darkness. Give us brave and generous hearts that we may live on the earth as good neighbours. O Sacred Heart of Jesus, we place our trust in you.

AT THE FIRESIDE:
Mary set out and went with haste to a Judaean town in the hill country, where she entered the house of Zechariah and greeted Elizabeth. (Luke 1:39-40)

Neighbours make journeys. They come in the morning before the postman delivers, just to check the water pipe and to catch up on the news. They come on foot across the hills because they know the skill of closing the distance.

Neighbours make journeys. They come at breakfast time and bring the milk for the porridge just to hear about the new baby and to begin the celebration. They come quietly through the back door because they know the skill of sharing.

Neighbours make journeys. They come at the waiting time and sit till the moon fades, listening to the ancient stories, telling new ones of faith and hope. They come comfortably to the fireside because they know the skill of gathering.

Neighbours make journeys. They come at the working time to give a day on the bog or at the threshing floor, lending a hand to make way for the harvest. They come with forks and spades because they know the skill of timing.

Neighbours make journeys. They come at wedding time to make a toast and dance an old time waltz, leaving money for a new beginning to help them on their way. They come when the visitors have left because they know the skill of friendship.

Neighbours make journeys. They come at funeral time and watch through the night until the light returns, holding the family together with a decade of the rosary. They come the day after and bring the homemade bread because they know the skill of comfort.

We Pray:

You came to me across the hills,
Thank you for being my neighbour.
You waited with me when the lights went out,
Thank you for being my neighbour.
You worked beside me and we dug together,
Thank you for being my neighbour.

O love of God in the heart of Jesus, you are the unity of human hearts and the special character of the neighbour's presence. We place our trust in your love as we make our journeys of peace. Amen.

IN THE NEIGHBOURHOOD:
In everything, do to others as you would have them do to you; for this is the law and the prophets. (Matthew 7:12)

The golden rule is written into the scriptures of all major religions. When Jesus taught the golden rule he gave us a yardstick for humanity, a fair measurement and a high standard. In deciding what is right for others we choose what is right for ourselves: 'That is the entire law, all the rest is commentary.'

The golden rule, unlike other rules, is of one's own making and it finds its definition in the way we live together. It does not prohibit behaviours, as rules usually do, but encourages them. It is not about what to avoid but it is about what to desire. Deciding not to do wrong is the thinking of small hearts; deciding to practise our highest ideals on others is the stuff of noble hearts. The qualitative difference here is between avoiding and doing.

The golden rule is still the hope of the universe. It offers the way of reconciliation between exploitation and respect, between labour and capital, between honesty and fraud. We have learned first-hand from our market economies how failures in respect, justice and care come back to haunt us. Disregard for the golden rule is a penalty against ourselves.

The golden rule comes alive in a particular way where neighbours live as friends. A neighbourhood is a training ground for give and take, where people practise the skill of passing the ball and sharing the glory. Neighbours excel in the golden rule because neighbours understand how loving works.

We Pray:

> Where there is hatred may love begin with me,
> Christ be in my vision and understanding.
> Where there is division may peace begin with me,
> Christ be in my vision and understanding.
> Where there is offence may forgiveness begin with me,
> Christ be in my vision and understanding.
>
> O love of God in the heart of Jesus, plant the golden rule
> in the secret of our hearts. May it inspire our giving and
> receiving in our families and in our neighbourhoods, that we
> may experience communion. Our trust, O God, is in your
> love. Amen.

A Neighbour's Prayer:

On this patch of earth that I call home, I have come to know the meaning of belonging and I have experienced the heart of friendship. May I be a good neighbour on life's journey, stopping to share a story, waiting to hear the news.

In this parish where I was anointed into the Christian Community, I have come to know the rhythm of a lived faith and I have experienced the prayer space. May I be a good neighbour on life's journey, lighting the candle of hope, offering a cup of tea.

In this town-land where sorrows and joys are shared, I have discovered friendship and I have experienced something unbreakable. May I be a good neighbour on life's journey, standing in solidarity beside you in your sad times and in your happy times.

On this village street where footprints merge and conversations have the buzz of life, I have grown to value companionship and I have experienced a mingling of energies. May I be a good neighbour on life's journey, sharing the work of human hands, blessing every hour.

On this country road where people wait for the birds and grasses to announce the seasons of life, I have learned about harmony and I have experienced the unity of life in field and forest. May I be a good neighbour on life's journey, feeding the robin and dancing in the meadow.

In this family where I get my name, my identity and my history, I have seen the generosity of loving and I have experienced the holy water. May I be a good neighbour on life's journey, holding a prayer for all families in the secret of my heart.

THE HEART WELCOMES

I cannot possess Christ just for myself; I can belong to him only in union with all those who have become, or who will become, his own.

(Deus caritas est, 14)

Visitors from the East:
*Where is the child who has been born King of the Jews? For we
have observed his star at its rising and have come to pay him
homage. (Matthew 2:3)*

Welcoming is the attitude of acceptance, the art of receiving.
We all depend on the hospitality of others to bring friendship
and warmth to our journey. From the time of Abraham the
people of ancient Israel understood that being the people of God
meant that they were a welcoming people. They were called to be
available to the stranger and the sojourner, to the prince and the
pauper.

The visit of the Magi from the East to welcome the King of
the Jews in Bethlehem resounds with the generosity of the giver
and the availability of the receiver. Here we see the transcendence
of ethnic, social and religious boundaries as dignitaries and kings
embrace. Welcoming is always about valuing and honouring.

Like ourselves, Jesus also depended on hospitality to realise
the purpose of his life. Where he was welcomed the seed of God's
love took root and where he was rejected the very dust from that
street was lost in the wind. When the Magi came carrying their
gifts they placed a star of welcome on the map of the universe.

Gift giving has always been a deeply personal way of saying
'welcome'. We offer gold, the best we have. We offer frankincense
because we are anointed people. We offer myrrh to herald the
final welcome when we pass through death into life. When the
Magi followed the star they led us to the meeting place.

We Pray:

> May we follow the star to the place of welcome,
> Jesus, you are welcome at our house.
> May we offer a gift to honour your presence,
> Jesus, you are welcome at our house.
> May we see in you the face of God,
> Jesus, you are welcome at our house.

> O love of God in the heart of Jesus, you welcome all the
> tribes of the earth to the place where you live. May we find
> the star in our time and may we travel together in friendship
> and in peace. Our trust, O God, is in your love. Amen.

VISITORS I SEND:
Whoever welcomes the one I send, welcomes me and whoever
welcomes me, welcomes the one who sent me. (John 13:20)

We are the Ireland of 'welcomes' and Irish people everywhere
still value and express this unique identity, because an Irish
welcome is an experience that is remembered. It is not of
economic benefit only, but more significantly it is a gift of character,
which reveals the soul of the nation. When we extend the hand
of welcome it is our finest hour.

Jesus was very conscious of welcoming and of being welcomed.
He stands at every door and knocks. He wears the postman's
hat and the milkman's coat and at times, the neighbour's boots.
He collects our refuse, borrows the lawnmower and calls for an
evening chat. Sometimes he speaks with a foreign accent but his
language is always international. It is never difficult to recognise
him because he bears a likeness to all people of good will. The
only thing that saddens him is a locked door; the only thing
that frightens him is a handshake withheld. He is at home in
the garden shed or in the front parlour and, as he sees it, the
abundant life is in the house of welcomes.

Jesus identified every welcome with the action and presence of God and he explained moments of welcome as encounters with God. He himself liked invitations, but it was the warm welcome, sometimes with tears, sometimes with bread and wine, that he wrote in the memory of his heart. It is understandable then that the 'fáilte' remains one of Ireland's remarkable wonders.

We Pray:

> For people who have no place to call home,
> Céad míle fáilte.
> For people who are rejected by systems of power,
> Céad míle fáilte.
> For people who are looking for a home in Ireland,
> Céad míle fáilte.

> O love of God in the heart of Jesus, you are the welcoming centre of the universe. Draw all people into your heart and may we be one in love. O Sacred Heart of Jesus we place our trust in you. Amen.

VISITORS WHO KEEP MY WORD:
Those who love me will keep my word, and my Father will love them, and we will come to them and make our home with them. (John 14:23)

Seasons come and seasons go; the waves rise and fall. People move from childhood to old age but the experience of home lasts for ever. There is no event in life to equal the experience of 'coming home'.

The people of ancient Israel learned the pain of separation from the homeland and their yearning for the House in Jerusalem led them home. For them home was an assurance of the presence of Yahweh, a living space to love and be loved. When Jesus spoke to us of sharing his home, he was offering us a timeless connection, a place in the family. Home is the dependable presence in every life.

Every home is a place of presence, a building with a heart. Here we are never locked out. The fireside chair, the breakfast stool, the kitchen table all say 'come in'. A home is not defined by timber and stone but has the shape of the people who live and love there. The familiar signs of the Sacred Heart lamp, the holy water font, and the shared meal have survived with every generation. And while we search for new images in our time, presence abides. Making a home is the achievement of hearts where the word of God resounds in the family gathering and where people live as one to keep the presence in the home.

Good homes are lighthouses of hope, reaching out to sea. Unlike the sand castle that is washed away on the changing tide, a good home holds together in the storm. Jesus promised us a home with him. He is going to take us with him, to the same address, to the place where he lives. To be at home is, ultimately, to belong, to be with God.

We Pray:

When we gather to celebrate our joy,
Make your home with us, O God.
When we gather to support and comfort each other,
Make your home with us, O God.
When we gather to share the bread and to remember,
Make your home with us, O God.

O love of God in the heart of Jesus, may we build homes where love is taught, where faith is caught and where the presence of each person is honoured. We make our prayer through Jesus, in whose love is our trust. Amen.

A Welcoming Prayer:

We welcome you to our home. May your stay with us be
happy and may Christ keep company with our time together.

We welcome you to our family. May our conversation with
you be loving and may Christ keep company with our
sharing.

We welcome you to our open fire. May you sit a while in
its warm embrace and may Christ keep company with our
fireside rest.

We welcome you to our gathering. May our companionship
be warm and life-giving and may Christ keep company with
our occasion.

We welcome you to our celebration. May our joy be full with
songs of thanksgiving and may Christ keep company with
our dancing.

We welcome you to our storytelling. May we tell of the
seasons, of bright days and of dark days and may Christ keep
company with our journey.

We welcome you to the soft chair. May you let go of your
burdens and find a space of ease and may Christ keep
company with our time of rest.

We welcome you to our meal. May our remembering be
of gifts received and of service given and may Christ keep
company with our communion.

THE HEART SEES

The Christian programme ... is 'a heart which sees'. This heart sees where love is needed and acts accordingly.

(Deus caritas est, 31b)

INTO ENEMY TERRITORY:
Love your enemies, do good to those who hate you, bless those who curse you, pray for those who abuse you. (Luke 6:27)

Love is the only single word that expresses the birth, life, death and resurrection of Jesus. It is the language of international exchange and of global renewal. It bridges centuries of division and sets free the winner and the loser. With Jesus, love becomes the regulator of the social order. He called us beyond rules and their measurements to freedom. This was a new way of engaging with life, of befriending enemies. Jesus understood love as the avenue for change and restoration. When he equated the Law to loving he expanded the human expression to infinity.

'Love your enemies.' The very concept opened a new landmark on the achievements of history. It was the language of a political and a cultural revolution. It evoked in us great and noble deeds, benevolent and generous decisions. We would love into life the people who sought to destroy us and by prayer and blessings we would repair hatred with love. Minimalism, bargains and sanctions were no longer effective options; something heroically human would be needed to take us over the finish line together.

The new system was expansive and beyond control. It disregarded logic and court rhetoric and went for the heart. The last were first and the weak were strong. The system keepers were out of step and the people left Egypt. Love changed everything and shut down death itself. That is his legacy. He bequeathed it to the system that sought to destroy him because in the secret of his heart he heard the impoverished cry from the enemy position. By this shall they surely know.

We Pray:

For families divided by power struggles,
Where there is hatred we will sow love.
For communities divided by memories of yesterday,
Where there is hatred we will sow love.
For nations divided by suspicion and competition,
Where there is hatred we will sow love.

O love of God in the heart of Jesus, you gave your love to
friend and foe, to sinner and to saint without counting the
cost. Pour your love into our hearts that we may build bridges
to enemy territory. We place all our trust in your love. Amen.

INTO A FATHER'S SORROW:
*My little daughter is at the point of death. Come and lay your
hands on her that she may get well. (Luke 8:40-56)*

Jairus, we assume had tried every medicinal remedy to save his
only child. As a leader in the synagogue who enjoyed prominence
and influence, his turning to Jesus for help was very significant.
Jairus needed someone who could enter the deepest anguish of
a human heart and feel the devastation of a father's grief. His
approach to Jesus was full of humility and faith, for Jairus knew
that he was crossing a great cultural and religious divide.

The encounter between Jesus and Jairus proclaims the Gospel
of universal salvation. Jesus will go to the other side and he will
plead before God the cause of the Jewish leader. Jairus too will
have to understand that he is crossing a threshold in his faith
journey into a community where equal status is given to all. The
lesson is made clear when Jesus stops to heal the unclean woman,
who by touching him has disregarded purity regulations.

Jesus appreciates the giant leap of faith that Jairus has taken
but the synagogue official will have to learn the way of absolute
trust, the art of waiting and of holding on to hope. Like all of us
he will learn that with Jesus, situations are never insurmountable

and it is never too late to pray. When Jesus eventually reached the house where the child was already dead, he touched the corpse and commanded life to return. The prayer of a father was heard that day, mending the ancient divisions, touching the heart of God: 'Do not fear; only believe and she will be saved.'

We Pray:

In times of great sorrow may our faith endure the pain,
Lord, increase our faith.
In times of doubt and fear may our faith endure the wait,
Lord, increase our faith.
In times of losing a child may our faith endure the death,
Lord, increase our faith.

O love of God in the heart of Jesus, you hear the prayer of the heart and it penetrates all barriers to reach you. Thank you for loving all people back to life and thank you for loving me. Our trust is in your love. Amen.

INTO A SYCAMORE TREE:
The half of my goods, Lord, I give to the poor, and if I have cheated anyone I will pay him back four times as much. (Luke 19:8)

Zacchaeus was a chief tax collector, a person of considerable wealth. His granary was full but his heart was impoverished and Zacchaeus knew that one can have the status of the rich and yet experience the poverty of the outcast. He had heard the grumble of respectability when Jesus associated with tax collectors, and fearing the public isolation of social rejection, he sought the safety of the sycamore tree to get a glimpse of the prophet who was passing that day.

Seeing Jesus was relatively easy, even for one of low stature, but as the story unfolds we find a man who desires more, a meeting maybe, perhaps a meal? Meeting Jesus, however, is always a challenging experience, mixed with difficult questions and radical choices. For Zacchaeus, the tax collector, there was a particular problem because his riches stood between him and rebirth. Discipleship brought consequences, and for Zacchaeus, leaving the treetop was a journey back to a community commissioned to bring good news to the poor.

The pursuit of a just and equitable society with a fair distribution of wealth was the choice that faced the chief tax collector. It was the requirement of discipleship then and now. Zacchaeus must return to ground level if he was to take his place beside the prophet who lifted up the lowly and set the downtrodden free. When Jesus looked into the sycamore tree he saw the heart of the man and he offered him a place on the team, an opportunity to become a new creation. Zacchaeus understood the implication of the invitation. He understood the relationship between eating the meal and sharing the meal. Zacchaeus left the sycamore tree that day.

We Pray:

My eyes are watching for you my God,
Hear O Lord and answer me.
My soul is searching for you, my God,
Hear O Lord and answer me.
My heart is longing for you, my God,
Hear O Lord and answer me.

O love of God in the heart of Jesus, you search the hiding place for us from one generation to the next and you lead us home. Help us to hear your call and return it, so that we may stay connected to your heart. All our trust is in your love. Amen.

A SEEKER'S PRAYER:

I am searching for you O God on the pebbled beach of time, among the footprints of the travellers where you made your home.

I am searching for you O God on the mighty rocks, fortress for the sea birds, where you prayed alone.

I am searching for you O God in the quiet sand dunes where the grasses protect the landscape against the crashing sea.

I am searching for you O God on the stormy waves as they rise and fall without losing their purpose.

I am searching for you O God on the flight of the seagull where courage lets go to the call of the ocean.

I am searching for you O God in the dance of the sunlight as it keeps time with the tides, moving towards infinity.

I am searching for you O God on the mountain slope as it rises above the waters, giving another perspective.

I am searching for you O God on the seabed as it holds the secrets of history, keeping the silence.

I am searching for you O God on the salted spray, as it balances life and death, holding the mystery.

I am searching for you O God from the treetop as it supports the climber's weight, revealing the seeker's destiny.

THE HEART CROSSES BOUNDARIES

*Love is indeed 'ecstasy', not in the sense of a moment
of intoxication but rather as a journey, an ongoing
exodus out of the closed inward-looking self towards its
liberation through self-giving, and thus towards authentic
self-discovery and indeed the discovery of God.*

(*Deus caritas est*, 6)

IN THE CATTLE SHED:
The shepherds returned giving praise and glory to God. (Luke 2:20)

Let us go and see the God who became one with his people. We will make the journey on foot that we may know the road crossing the time boundary between heaven and earth. Let us go with haste for this is an unrepeatable moment, the one we must not miss. In the silence of our expectation may we hear the voice of angels and their tidings of great joy. Tonight the mystery intensifies. A saviour is born for us! The heart of God has crossed the desert of separation, to become our lifeline. Let us go over to Bethlehem.

In the birth of this child, history becomes purposeful and time becomes eternal. The calendar of our days is now a heart event, marking the birthday of all creation. As our direction turns to Bethlehem, we discover the child wrapped in swaddling cloths. Love is vulnerable and human, fragile and humble. Its only empire is the shelter where people gather for the Passover. Its only ambition is to speak to other hearts. The ox and the ass are close by for they too have recognised their moment. Their breath mingles with human breath to acclaim the end of boundaries.

The one we have waited for is here. He is the face of God's love for the king and the shepherd, for the beast and the grasses. His smallness fills the empty space and time merges in the starlight as he sets his face to carry us across the divide. He is with us now and will be with us to the end, leading us from the cattle shed into the new Jerusalem.

We Pray:

> May our time in Bethlehem lead us to God,
> A child is born for us.
> May our achievement in life be loving relationships,
> A child is born for us.
> May our understanding of life be love,
> A child is born for us.

O love of God in the heart of Jesus, in you all time is God's time. It was your love that broke into human space and connected the worlds of beginnings and endings. With love you unlocked the closed door and revealed the entrance code. All our trust is in your love. Amen.

IN THE JORDAN:

Then Jesus came from Galilee to John at the Jordan, to be baptised by him. (Matthew 2:13)

Love and hospitality go together. The Jordan River still flows in the land of Jesus' birth. In the secret of its heart the river remembers the days of Joshua and how it provided a passageway to the Promised Land. It remembers the bodies that were healed and the hearts that were restored. The day of christening began in a great exodus of people from their villages, pouring into the valley searching for living water. The air was heavy with expectation and as they immersed in the waters they asked that they might belong. They yearned for words of welcome, to be received into the family of Jesus.

As the waters of the ancient river covered their pilgrim bodies the voice of John announced the 'Lamb of God'. He was making his way to the Jordan to go down with the masses, to sink his own heart into the anguish of human hunger. He had come to welcome them, to become one of the pilgrims, to enfold them in the hospitality of God. It was an anointing moment and the Spirit of God broke through the heavens and hovered over the water imprinting a divine seal on the people who had followed the Lamb.

This was the company of God and the Father, and the Spirit proclaimed the Son as the one who would take the people safely through the water. The greater and lesser lights yielded to the new dawn and the void resounded with expectation as the Son was named. Love had come into the Jordan and the river washed away the boundaries and sealed the peoples' identity in a new covenant.

We Pray:

In Baptism you give us the keys to your house,
Holy Spirit, breathe your life in us.
In Baptism you wash us in the waters of freedom,
Holy Spirit, breathe your life in us.
In Baptism you cross boundaries to save us,
Holy Spirit, breathe your life in us.

O love of God in the heart of Jesus, you crossed the great divide to meet us at the water. Your love flows freely from the heart of the Lamb. May all who long for freedom come to the water and may your torrents wash over us and your love invade our beings. Our trust is in your love. Amen.

IN THE VALLEY:
I am the Good Shepherd. The Good Shepherd lays down his life for the sheep. (John 10:11)

The news of heroic actions usually captures the public imagination. We have heard of people who jumped into rivers, risked gunfire, returned to burning buildings for the life of another person. That's what good shepherds do; they follow their hearts. When Jesus called himself the Good Shepherd he had captives and outcasts on his mind, those fettered and at risk. He knew about recovery missions and how he would have to cross boundaries of prejudice and social distinctions and work through the night to untangle the undergrowth and let the sheep go free.

Inclusion is the way of the good shepherd. He knows the names and personalities, the habits and qualities of his sheep. He knows where they were last seen and where they are most likely to be. He is not concerned about the rules of fencing and ethnic rituals and neither Jerusalem nor Rome will confine his discovery. The Good Shepherd understands inclusion as the ethos of the sheepfold. He grasps the magnificence of diversity, the secret of the rainbow and he negotiates every boundary until the colours merge and the covenant is signed.

When the sheep gather at the evening hour, the Good Shepherd is alert for the ones who did not come home. He is anxious for those left behind in the traffic jam, for those pushed off the road by speed and competition and for those who took the wrong turn. Inclusion is integral in the sheepfold and so he sets out while the world sleeps to find the tax collectors who are in hiding and the lepers who are unwanted. It is an arduous journey, taking on the current of public opinion and crossing landmines of human verdicts. But the Good Shepherd knows his sheep and he hears the secret of every heart.

We Pray:

Lord, stay with us on the hillside, and keep us from sliding,
You are the Good Shepherd.
Lord, walk with us in the valleys and keep us from falling,
You are the Good Shepherd.
Lord, wait for us at the sheepfold and welcome us home,
You are the Good Shepherd.

O love of God in the heart of Jesus, you follow us all the days of our lives with goodness and kindness, and despite the lost times you will bring us safely home. All our trust is in your love. Amen.

A Traveller's Prayer:

O guardian angel, sent by God to guide and protect me, lead me on the road as you once led Israel.

O guardian angel, given authority by God, watch over me when I move and when I lie down.

O guardian angel, present with Daniel in the lion's den, stay close to me in my hour of danger.

O guardian angel, messenger of God, make your way to my house as you once made your way to Nazareth.

O guardian angel, defender of God's people, plead my cause before the throne of God.

O guardian angel, companion of the traveller, accompany me on the highways and on the byways.

O guardian angel, standing at the throne of God, offer a prayer for my safe arrival.

O guardian angel, member of the heavenly choir, sing to me of the glory of God.

O guardian angel, faithful friend of my journey, hold my hand on the ascent and in the descent.

O guardian angel, you lit up the sky in Bethlehem, be a star of wonder in my night sky.

O guardian angel, you supported Jesus in the desert, wait beside me when I am broken and afraid.

O guardian angel, you stayed with Jesus in his hour of agony, sit with me when I am betrayed by those I trusted most.

O guardian angel, you announced the empty tomb and the dawn for all creation, lead me to my place in the choir.

THE HEART KNOWS GOD

God's love for us is fundamental for our lives, and it raises the important question about who God is and who we are.

(Deus caritas est, 2)

AT THE BEGINNING:
Master, now you are dismissing your servant in peace, according to your word; for my eyes have seen your salvation. (Luke 2:29)

I am Simeon. I was brought up in a deeply religious Jewish environment where people spoke of a promised Messiah. The very idea was enthralling to me and it filled the dreams of my youth. I read from Isaiah and I listened intently to the unfolding story. When Jesus was born there were rumours and contradictions, but as early as the night of his birth, a few shepherds on a hillside outside Bethlehem reported news of a Saviour! I was much too old to go over to Bethlehem but I followed the star as it moved over the temple.

On the eighth day after his birth, I was led by the Spirit into the temple. I was familiar with the Spirit directing the events of my life, and when I saw the young mother and father with their infant son, I reached out my hand to bless the child. Mary handed the infant to me and that was the moment when my eyes opened and my waiting ended and my life was complete.

I was an old man and I was holding the child. A new presence was entering the temple and we could sense it. The prophetess, Anna, had also waited a lifetime for the hour of revelation and our waiting was our witness to the promise of God. At the temple that day there was an ending and a beginning, and the old man and the child were instruments in the story of salvation to the ends of the earth.

Israel's story was verified before my very eyes and my life's purpose was fulfilled. Jesus would extend his influence beyond Israel, for he was also a light to the Gentiles, a prophet for the universe. Mary and Joseph were astonished at my words and I tried to explain that the heart recognises God.

We Pray:

> Keep us waiting in hope, O God,
> Show us your salvation.
> Help us to recognise the light, O God,
> Show us your salvation.
> Lead us to your Son, O God,
> Show us your salvation.

> O love of God in the heart of Jesus, you brought the hope
> of salvation to a waiting universe. May we, like Simeon,
> open our arms to your coming and may our hearts come to
> recognise you. Our trust is in your love. Amen.

ON THE ROAD:
Were not our hearts burning within us? (Luke 24:32)

He spoke to us on the road of the woman who gave birth to him in a village of no significance and of his Baptism with sinners all seeking a common purpose. He found friendship in the tavern and in the temple, with shepherds and with kings, and he acknowledged the cause of everyone he met, reading the heart, forgiving the blindness.

He described street corners where he had waited to make contact and hillsides where thousands gathered for bread and water. He wrote their names, every one of them in the secret of his heart. With his strong shoulder he transported the wounded to a place of rest; with his great arm he reached beyond the edge to rescue the climber and to save the lost sheep.

He remembered how he worked tirelessly with his shepherd's staff to rescue dying systems and how he immersed himself in human darkness until the dawn broke. He reinterpreted the Law despite mounting opposition from Church and State, and as his accusers closed in on him the stones began to cry out and the people waved freedom branches. When he promised to destroy death for ever and to rise again from the grave there were accusations of blasphemy, but the earth had already begun to move.

With courage and compassion he reversed the social order and the lowly and the mighty were connected in a river of life. From the channel of his mercy he gave every weed an invitation to blossom and every fig tree a second chance. He heard every story, spoken and unspoken and he forgave seventy times seven until he repaid our debts with his flesh and blood. On the road our own hearts burned within us as he revealed the heart of God.

We Pray:

> Jesus, walk beside us and help us to remember,
> Come in and stay with us.
> Jesus, help us to hear the story again,
> Come in and stay with us.
> Jesus, show us the heart of God,
> Come in and stay with us.

> O love of God in the heart of Jesus, be our companion
> on life's journey. Speak to us of God's love and may your
> friendship be a fire burning in our hearts. Amen.

AT THE END:
Surely this man was God's Son! (Mark 15:39)

I was puzzled when the sentence was given. I had always believed in 'beyond reasonable doubt' and our legal system seemed once again to dismiss the vulnerable one. I was relieved, however, when he eventually took the cross on his shoulder. At last we were on our way and the day would end early for criminals and soldiers alike.

I was frustrated when he went down but I did notice how slow he was to respond to the whip. There was something oddly patient about him, a man without a grumble. I was a bit emotional when his mother appeared. She was so helpless and so bewildered that her voice had no sound. However, she stood bravely beside him with a gentle pride that mothers always carry for their children. It did occur to me as she carried the cross with him that she too knew the seriousness of this injustice.

I was grateful to Simon; he speeded things up. His first reaction on being publicly associated with another man's crime was one of anger. Since I was the one who plucked Simon from the crowd I watched him carefully. As he stumbled along carrying the weight of another man's cross, his anger seemed to abate and his face softened and his hands began to embrace the wood. When we eventually took the cross from Simon, he asked me if he could continue to the top of the hill just to be there to the end. My gratitude to Simon was turning to amazement.

I was annoyed with Veronica. Women have a way of fussing and introducing unnecessary details. What good was a towel anyway at this point? When Veronica raised the towel to Jesus' face he seemed to lean forward and as I saw it, she was holding the weight of his grief in her hands. As Veronica withdrew, Jesus looked deeply into her eyes as if to say that this single act of kindness was indelible.

I couldn't believe it when Jesus went down a second time. Our whips were silent now because we feared that he might die on the road. Instead I offered him my arm and when he uttered 'thank you', my whole body trembled with tenderness. In that instant I feared that the Roman soldier was wavering.

I had heard women wailing many times before and this display failed to impress me either. Jesus, however, used the moment to break his silence. They should be weeping 'For themselves and for their children', he said. Was he linking this death journey to future generations? A question began to beat in my heart.

I was silent at the third fall. Jesus was losing blood and his eyes were fixed in pain. As he looked into my face I had an unbelievable urge to hold him, to carry him, even to change sides for him. The very thought filled me with terror. What was happening to me?

I was uncomfortable when they removed his clothes with such violence and disregard. Whoever he was, he was a man of extraordinary dignity and I felt that in stripping him we were actually stripping the glory of Rome.

I was angry at the nailing. Enough is enough! I felt with every hammer blow that we had lost the day. We were hammering the indestructible, nailing the innocent. I didn't cry out; I just stood back.

I was crying when he died. My tears were full with relief and flowing with belief. I cried as I never cried before. I was free of the Empire. He spoke from the cross that day, deep human words of compassion and forgiveness and promise. I saw the heart of the man hanging on the cross and I knew that I was on holy ground. Surely, he was the Son of God!

We Pray:

Give me wisdom O God to see beyond the system,
Surely this man was the Son of God.
Give me courage O God to speak against injustice,
Surely this man was the Son of God.
Give me faith O God to see with the eyes of my heart,
Surely this man was the Son of God.

O love of God in the heart of Jesus, you break through barriers of hatred and blindness to restore in us the breath of life. You dissolve the steel of our armour until we lay down our swords. Thank you for never giving up on us. Our trust is in your love. Amen.

PRAYER TO THE SACRED HEART:

Heart of Jesus, present at the first light
We place our trust in you.

Heart of Jesus, pathway of the moving stars
We place our trust in you.

Heart of Jesus, tabernacle of God's presence
We place our trust in you.

Heart of Jesus, vision of the prophets' wisdom
We place our trust in you.

Heart of Jesus, glory of the human image
We place our trust in you.

Heart of Jesus, blood of the new covenant
We place our trust in you.

Heart of Jesus, channel of the people's prayer
We place our trust in you.

Heart of Jesus, generosity of the forgiving word
We place our trust in you.

Heart of Jesus, shape of the Christian gathering
We place our trust in you.

Heart of Jesus, sustenance of the family circle
We place our trust in you.

Heart of Jesus, strength of the darkest hour
We place our trust in you.

Heart of Jesus, bridge on the horizon of history
We place our trust in you.

Heart of Jesus, Heart of God
We place our trust in you.